STÉPHANE
FRATTINI

THE GREAT BIG ANIMAL SEARCH BOOK

LOM ART

CAN YOU FIND?

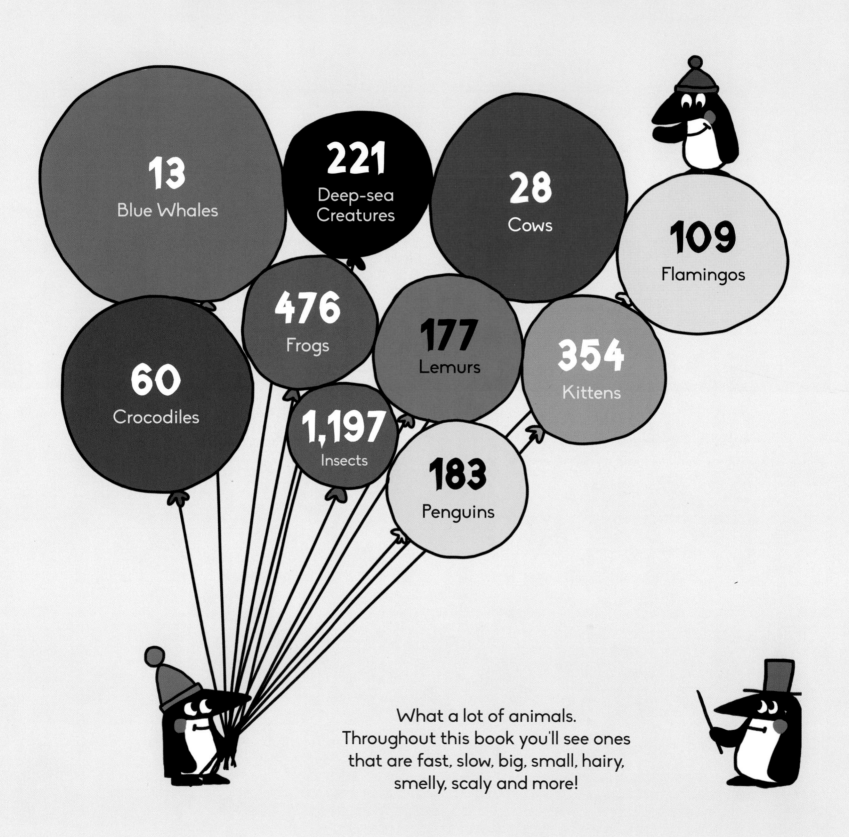

13 Blue Whales

221 Deep-sea Creatures

28 Cows

109 Flamingos

476 Frogs

60 Crocodiles

177 Lemurs

354 Kittens

1,197 Insects

183 Penguins

What a lot of animals.
Throughout this book you'll see ones
that are fast, slow, big, small, hairy,
smelly, scaly and more!

HERE'S YOUR CHALLENGE

This book is bursting with great big, beautiful bunches of animals.
There's loads of them, tons of them, lots and lots and lots ...

In fact there are over **2,800** creatures – from cuddly kittens and cute lemurs to
munching cows and mysterious creatures of the deep sea.

It's your job to find over **100** particular animals and objects
hidden among them, using the clues to help you.
Are you up to the challenge?

While you are searching, you'll come across fascinating facts about animals,
including how long they live, how much they eat, how much they weigh
and much, much more.

You'll also find out some of the special words used to describe
groups of animals – there's a '**waddle**' of penguins, a '**pod**' of whales and
a '**float**' of crocodiles. These weird words are called '**collective nouns**',
and they are some of the most wonderful phrases you can learn.

NOW IT'S TIME TO SEARCH AND FIND
ANIMALS OF EVERY KIND ...

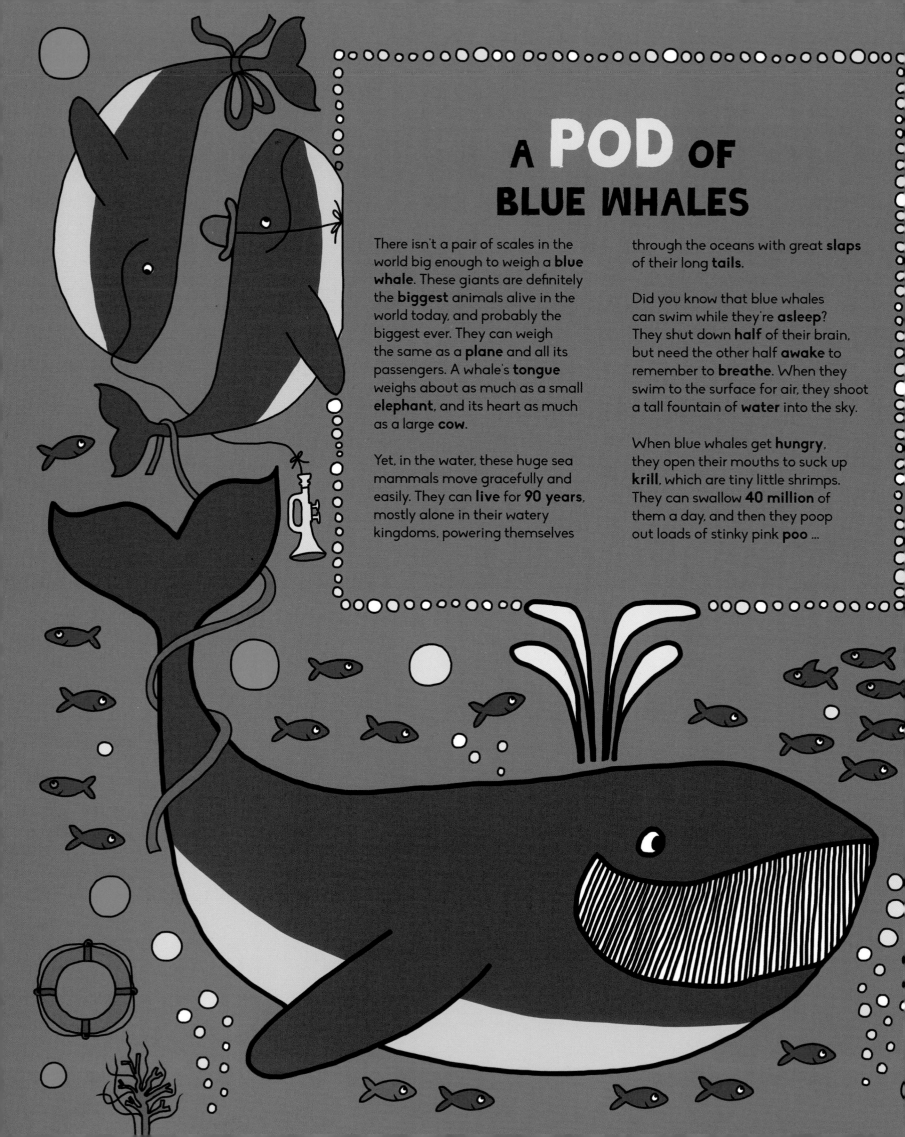

A POD OF BLUE WHALES

There isn't a pair of scales in the world big enough to weigh a **blue whale**. These giants are definitely the **biggest** animals alive in the world today, and probably the biggest ever. They can weigh the same as a **plane** and all its passengers. A whale's **tongue** weighs about as much as a small **elephant**, and its heart as much as a large **cow**.

Yet, in the water, these huge sea mammals move gracefully and easily. They can **live** for **90 years**, mostly alone in their watery kingdoms, powering themselves through the oceans with great **slaps** of their long **tails**.

Did you know that blue whales can swim while they're **asleep**? They shut down **half** of their brain, but need the other half **awake** to remember to **breathe**. When they swim to the surface for air, they shoot a tall fountain of **water** into the sky.

When blue whales get **hungry**, they open their mouths to suck up **krill**, which are tiny little shrimps. They can swallow **40 million** of them a day, and then they poop out loads of stinky pink **poo** ...

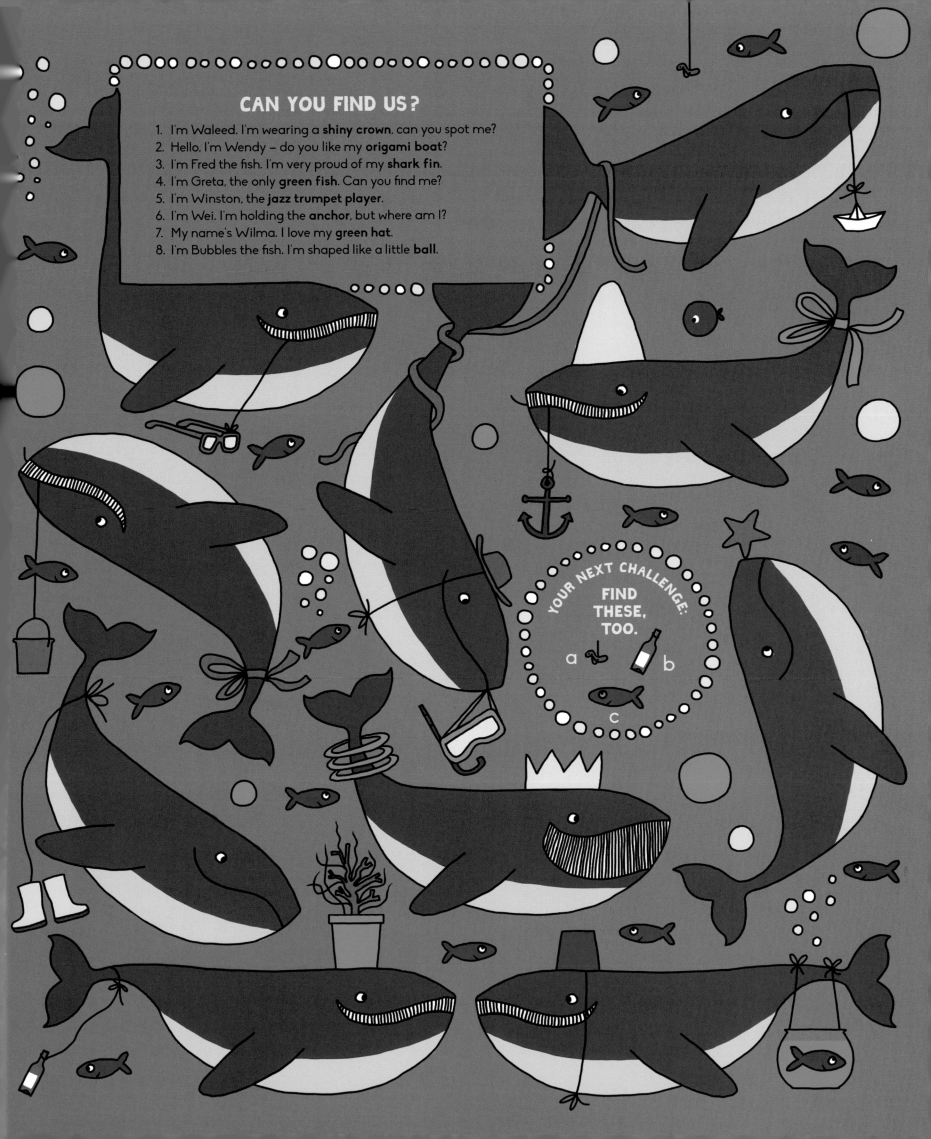

CAN YOU FIND US?

1. I'm Waleed. I'm wearing a **shiny crown**, can you spot me?
2. Hello, I'm Wendy – do you like my **origami boat**?
3. I'm Fred the fish. I'm very proud of my **shark fin**.
4. I'm Greta, the only **green fish**. Can you find me?
5. I'm Winston, the **jazz trumpet player**.
6. I'm Wei. I'm holding the **anchor**, but where am I?
7. My name's Wilma. I love my **green hat**.
8. I'm Bubbles the fish. I'm shaped like a little **ball**.

YOUR NEXT CHALLENGE:
FIND
THESE,
TOO.

a   b

c

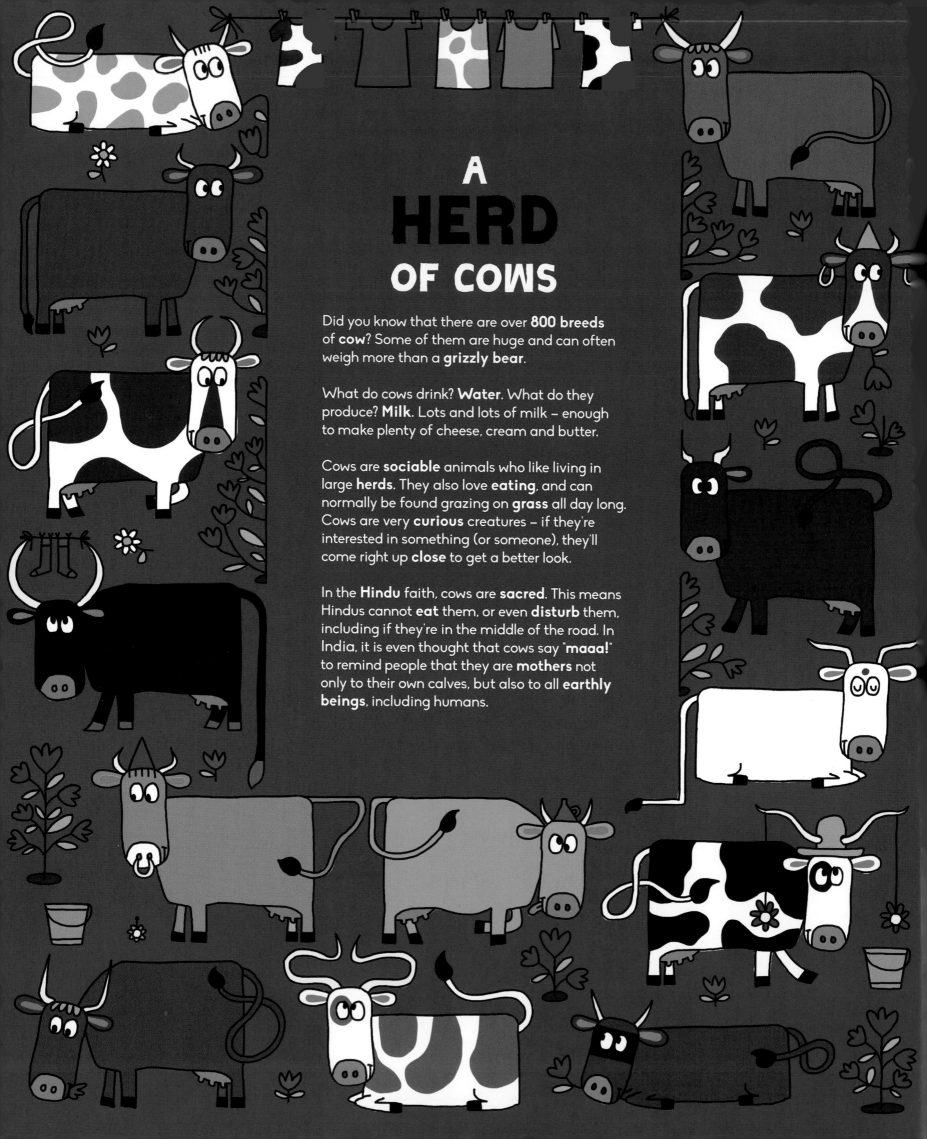

A HERD OF COWS

Did you know that there are over **800 breeds** of **cow**? Some of them are huge and can often weigh more than a **grizzly bear**.

What do cows drink? **Water**. What do they produce? **Milk**. Lots and lots of milk – enough to make plenty of cheese, cream and butter.

Cows are **sociable** animals who like living in large **herds**. They also love **eating**, and can normally be found grazing on **grass** all day long. Cows are very **curious** creatures – if they're interested in something (or someone), they'll come right up **close** to get a better look.

In the **Hindu** faith, cows are **sacred**. This means Hindus cannot **eat** them, or even **disturb** them, including if they're in the middle of the road. In India, it is even thought that cows say "**maaa!**" to remind people that they are **mothers** not only to their own calves, but also to all **earthly beings**, including humans.

GOOD LUCK SPOTTING US IN THE FIELD.

1. I'm Carlo, and I have a **map** of **Africa** on my coat.
2. Hello, my name's Cora. I only have **one ear**.
3. I'm Caterina. I've bought a new **hat**, but it's hiding my horns.
4. I'm Klara, can you find **me** and my **missing earring**?
5. I'm easy to spot — I'm Claude, the cow with the most **patches**.
6. My name is Charlie. Can you see if my **socks** are dry?
7. I'm Coco, and I love sticking out my **tongue**.
8. Hello, I'm Clemmie. I'm the only cow with **five hooves**.

YOUR NEXT CHALLENGE: **FIND THESE THINGS.**

a b c

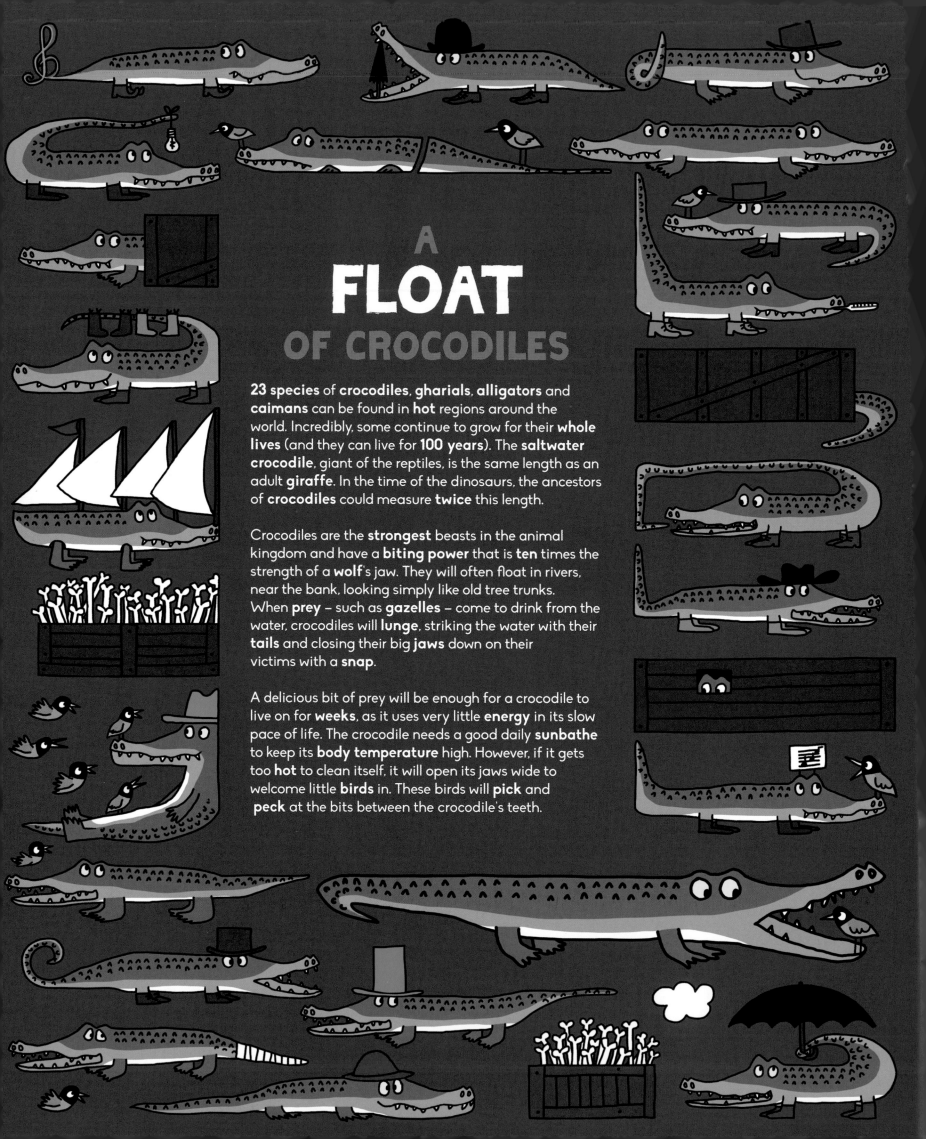

A
FLOAT
OF CROCODILES

23 species of **crocodiles**, **gharials**, **alligators** and **caimans** can be found in **hot** regions around the world. Incredibly, some continue to grow for their **whole lives** (and they can live for **100 years**). The **saltwater crocodile**, giant of the reptiles, is the same length as an adult **giraffe**. In the time of the dinosaurs, the ancestors of **crocodiles** could measure **twice** this length.

Crocodiles are the **strongest** beasts in the animal kingdom and have a **biting power** that is **ten** times the strength of a **wolf**'s jaw. They will often float in rivers, near the bank, looking simply like old tree trunks. When **prey** – such as **gazelles** – come to drink from the water, crocodiles will **lunge**, striking the water with their **tails** and closing their big **jaws** down on their victims with a **snap**.

A delicious bit of prey will be enough for a crocodile to live on for **weeks**, as it uses very little **energy** in its slow pace of life. The crocodile needs a good daily **sunbathe** to keep its **body temperature** high. However, if it gets too **hot** to clean itself, it will open its jaws wide to welcome little **birds** in. These birds will **pick** and **peck** at the bits between the crocodile's teeth.

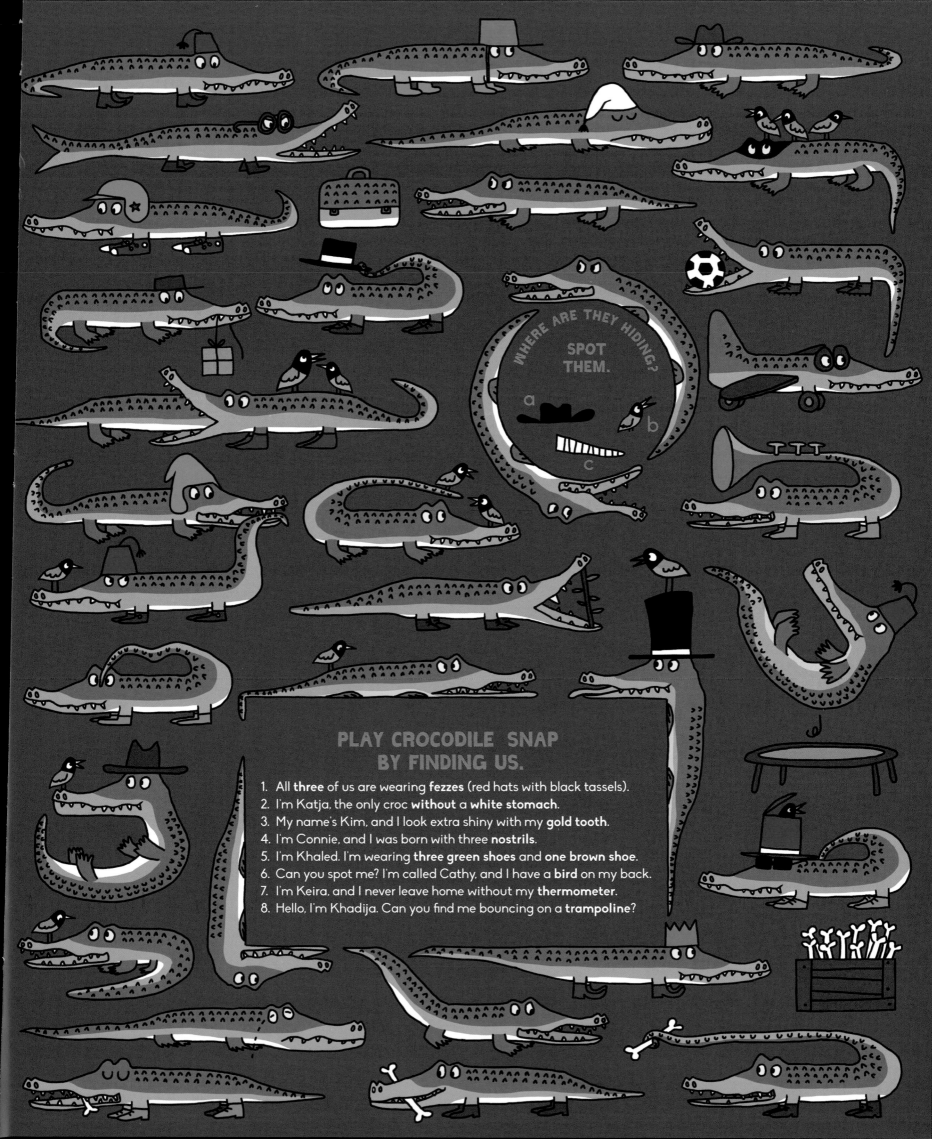

WHERE ARE THEY HIDING? SPOT THEM.

a
b
c

PLAY CROCODILE SNAP
BY FINDING US.

1. All **three** of us are wearing **fezzes** (red hats with black tassels).
2. I'm Katja, the only croc **without** a **white stomach**.
3. My name's Kim, and I look extra shiny with my **gold tooth**.
4. I'm Connie, and I was born with three **nostrils**.
5. I'm Khaled. I'm wearing **three green shoes** and **one brown shoe**.
6. Can you spot me? I'm called Cathy, and I have a **bird** on my back.
7. I'm Keira, and I never leave home without my **thermometer**.
8. Hello, I'm Khadija. Can you find me bouncing on a **trampoline**?

WHERE ARE THEY?
CAN YOU SPOT THEM?

a   b   c

FIND US BEFORE WE FLY AWAY.

1. I'm Farrah and both my feet have ended up in the same **clog**.
2. My name is Fred, and today I'm wearing my **snorkelling** gear.
3. Whoops! I'm Fletcher, I've swallowed my **star sheriff's badge**.
4. I'm Flo, and I've lost a **red boot**. My friend Fionn has **found** it, but where are we?
5. I'm Flavia, can you spot me? My **beak** is the **wrong way up.**
6. My name's Phillip. Spot me carrying a **white walking stick.**
7. Hello, I'm Fabio. You can find me by my **red crest** and **yellow feet.**
8. We're Flip, Flap and Flop. We're wearing **three necklaces** each.

A
FLAMBOYANCE
OF FLAMINGOS

With their long legs and necks, and their light, frilly feathers, groups of **flamingos** on the move share some similarities with **ballet dancers**.

Flamingos jabber and honk as they pick their way along the shore, heads dipped to filter the water and the mud with their specially-formed, curved **beaks**. They like to eat tiny **shrimps**, which are full of a substance called 'carotene'. This gives the birds their **pink** appearance – their feathers are originally **white**.

There are around **600,000** of these beautiful birds in the world. They are very light – the entire species is scarcely the weight of **four** large **planes** and all their passengers ...

Flamingos can **sleep** standing on **one** leg, and can hold this position effortlessly. This allows them to **fly away** easily if they sense **danger** or when it's time to **migrate** along with the rest of their flock in winter. "**See you next year!**" the flamingos cry, as they take off for warmer **climates**.

YOUR NEXT CHALLENGE:
FIND THEM.

a
b
c

FIND US IN THE SNOW,
BUT DON'T GET IN A FLAP ...

1. Can you spot us? We're the **four dads** keeping our eggs warm.
2. I'm Paddy. I'm excited as the shell of my egg has just **cracked**.
3. I'm Paul. I've just come back from a **fishing trip** with a **carrot**.
4. Vroom! I'm Parminder. Do you like my **little red car**?
5. My name's Phoebe and you can find me on my **unicycle**.
6. I'm Piper. Can you spot the beautiful **star** on my head?
7. Hello, I'm called Polly. I'm off to my first **guitar** lesson, wish me luck.
8. I'm Pablo. What do you think of my new **trainers**?

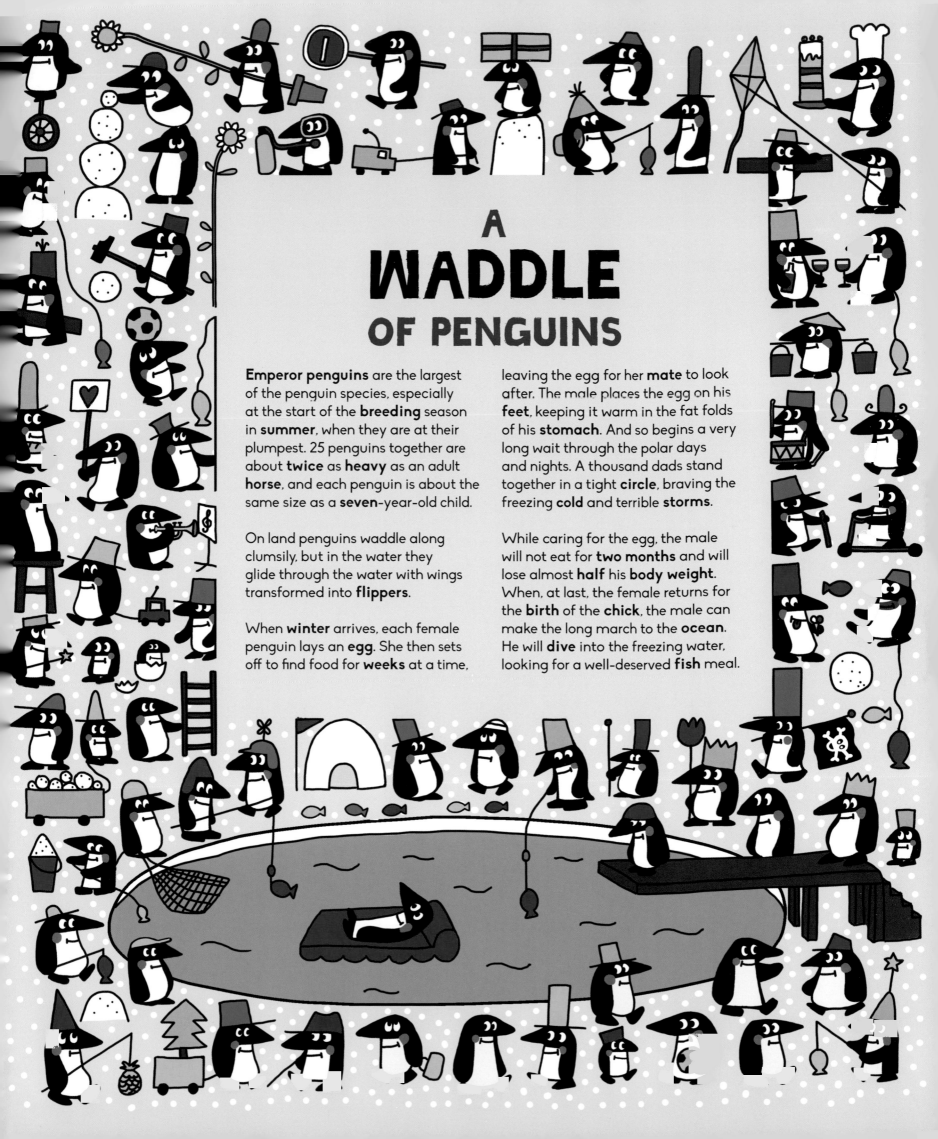

A
WADDLE
OF PENGUINS

Emperor penguins are the largest of the penguin species, especially at the start of the **breeding** season in **summer**, when they are at their plumpest. 25 penguins together are about **twice** as **heavy** as an adult **horse**, and each penguin is about the same size as a **seven**-year-old child.

On land penguins waddle along clumsily, but in the water they glide through the water with wings transformed into **flippers**.

When **winter** arrives, each female penguin lays an **egg**. She then sets off to find food for **weeks** at a time, leaving the egg for her **mate** to look after. The male places the egg on his **feet**, keeping it warm in the fat folds of his **stomach**. And so begins a very long wait through the polar days and nights. A thousand dads stand together in a tight **circle**, braving the freezing **cold** and terrible **storms**.

While caring for the egg, the male will not eat for **two months** and will lose almost **half** his **body weight**. When, at last, the female returns for the **birth** of the **chick**, the male can make the long march to the **ocean**. He will **dive** into the freezing water, looking for a well-deserved **fish** meal.

A CONSPIRACY
OF LEMURS

Ring-tailed lemurs are about the same size as **cats**, and are just as quick on their **feet**. With **eyes** like yellow marbles and zebra-striped **tails**, they are the best known members of the lemur family.

Lemur groups wake up at **dawn**, their movements shaking the trees they've slept in overnight. There are around **20** of them in each group, and they're led by a **matriarch** – an older female.

They will spend the day looking for tender **leaves**, **berries** and ripe **fruit**. Lemurs stay **together** on the move,

sticking their tails up to **communicate** with each other in the high grass, howling and purring as they go.

Ring-tailed lemurs have a fine sense of **smell** and the males mark their **territory** with strong **scents**. In the **mating** season, they even have **stink battles**: a lemur will rub its tail against its **scent glands** and wag it at his opponent. The lemur that is the most disgusted by the smell **runs away**.

Fights are rare, however, as the lemurs mostly enjoy **sitting** on the **ground** in the sun, warming themselves up before they go off to look for **food**.

CAN YOU FIND US?

1. I'm Lena. I love going fast on my **scooter**.
2. I'm Lamar. Can you find me on my **skateboard**?
3. We're Lily and Lisa. We're making a **heart**, to show our love.
4. My name's Leroy, and I'm known for lifting heavy **weights**.
5. I'm Lucy, a lemur **superhero**. Can you spot my **yellow cape**?
6. Hello, I'm Leilah. I like to keep my **sunglasses** on all day.
7. I'm Louis. I'm sticking out my **tongue** at the **bird** on my head.
8. I'm Luca, the **television** star. Can you find me?

WHERE ARE THEY? **FIND THEM.**

a

b

c

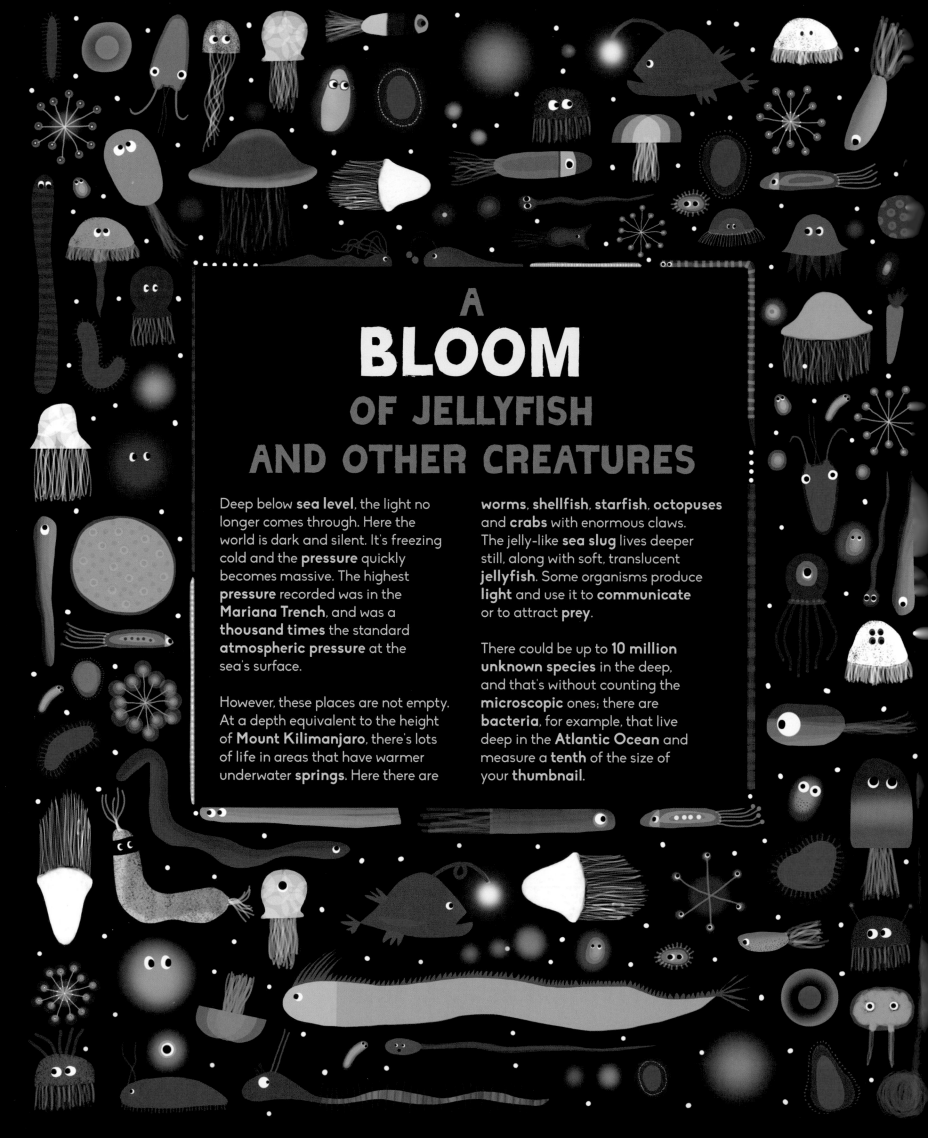

A BLOOM
OF JELLYFISH
AND OTHER CREATURES

Deep below **sea level**, the light no longer comes through. Here the world is dark and silent. It's freezing cold and the **pressure** quickly becomes massive. The highest **pressure** recorded was in the **Mariana Trench**, and was a **thousand times** the standard **atmospheric pressure** at the sea's surface.

However, these places are not empty. At a depth equivalent to the height of **Mount Kilimanjaro**, there's lots of life in areas that have warmer underwater **springs**. Here there are **worms**, **shellfish**, **starfish**, **octopuses** and **crabs** with enormous claws. The jelly-like **sea slug** lives deeper still, along with soft, translucent **jellyfish**. Some organisms produce **light** and use it to **communicate** or to attract **prey**.

There could be up to **10 million unknown species** in the deep, and that's without counting the **microscopic** ones; there are **bacteria**, for example, that live deep in the **Atlantic Ocean** and measure a **tenth** of the size of your **thumbnail**.

WHERE ARE WE HIDING?
SPOT US.

a   b
c

CAN YOU FIND US
IN THE DARKNESS?

1. We're Jamal and Jess, and we're making a **question mark**.
2. I'm Jonny. Find me by my **red glasses**.
3. My name is Jayden. Watch out for my **five pointed teeth**.
4. I'm Jack, and I never go out without my **mask**. Can you find me?
5. Hello, I'm Julia. I'm the only **star-shaped** creature.
6. I'm Crunchie. I'm a **carrot** that has been dropped into the sea.
7. My name is Jonas and I'm **white** with **four eyes**.
8. Greetings! I'm called Jasper. I'm **white** and I have a big **smile**.

A KINDLE
OF KITTENS

The cute house **cat** belongs to one of about **36** existing species of felines. Its first ancestors lived around **50 million years** ago, compared to the **four million years** that people have been around.

About **9,000 years** ago in Africa, a wild cat was first **tamed** by humans. Since then, the feline population has dramatically **increased**, and there are around **500 million** cats in the world today, including strays.

Cats start out their lives as **kittens**. Kittens are completely **helpless** when they are born, as they cannot **see**, **hear** or keep themselves **warm**. During their first week alive they spend **90 per cent** of their time sleeping. At about **eight days** old, kittens start to open their eyes. At **20 days** old they start learning the important skill of **hunting**. Then, at **eight weeks** old, kittens are able to look after themselves.

Some cats are **nocturnal**, and others prefer to spend evenings snoring away on someone's knee. The more **active** ones go **hunting** for **prey** in the garden and beyond, while some prefer to simply wait for **food** from their owners.

YOUR NEXT CHALLENGE:
FIND
THESE
THINGS.

a

b

c

CAN YOU FIND
WHERE WE ARE HIDING?

1. I'm Catherine, and I love my **bright red hoop**.
2. We're Kris and Karl. We always jump together on the **trampoline**.
3. My name's Kate, and I'm playing with my **skipping rope**.
4. I'm Carlotta. I'm hiding under my **black hat** – can you find me?
5. Boo! I'm Chandu, and I'm pretending to be a **ghost**.
6. I'm Kylie, the avenger. I've got my **black mask** on.
7. My name is Cookie. Can you give me a push on the **swing**?
8. I'm Kai, and I have a beautiful new **hat**. It's **red**, with a **white pompom** on it.

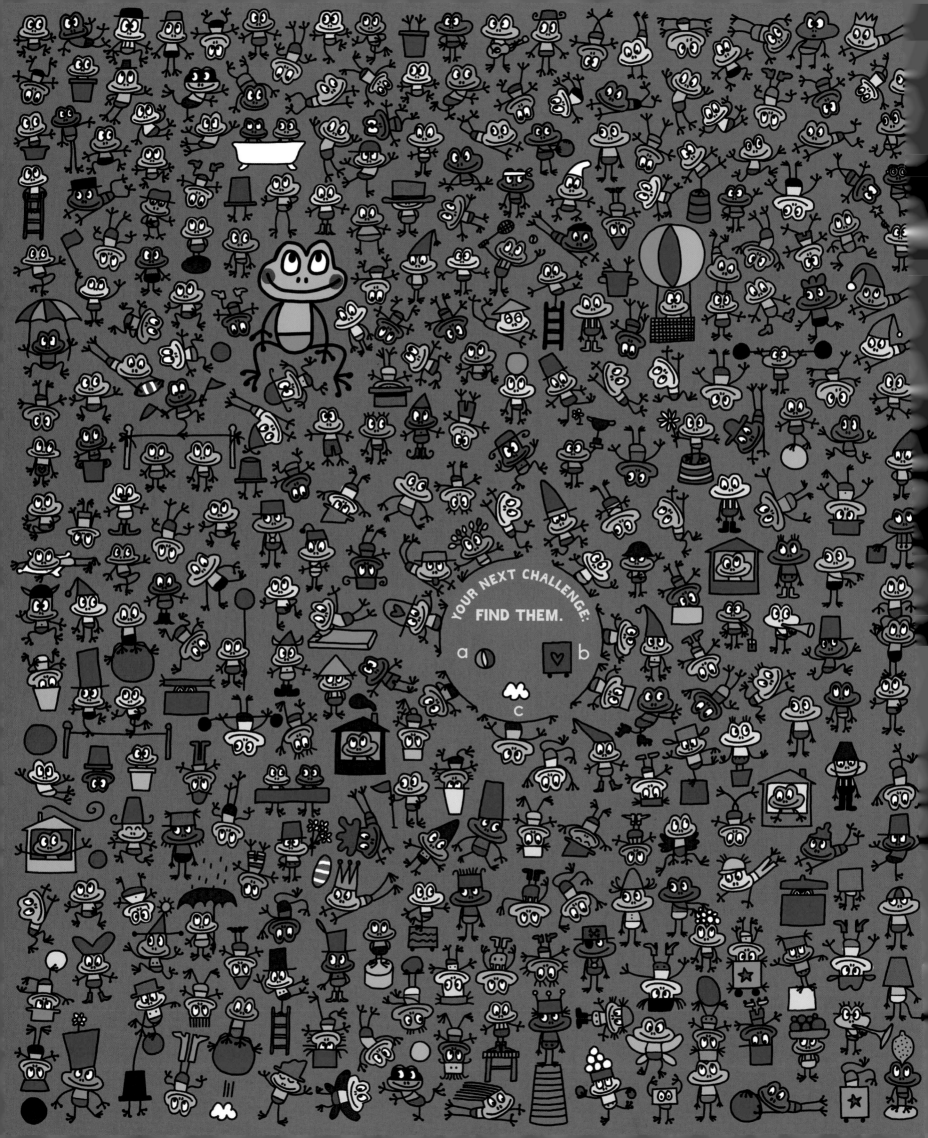

YOUR NEXT CHALLENGE:
FIND THEM.

a   b

c

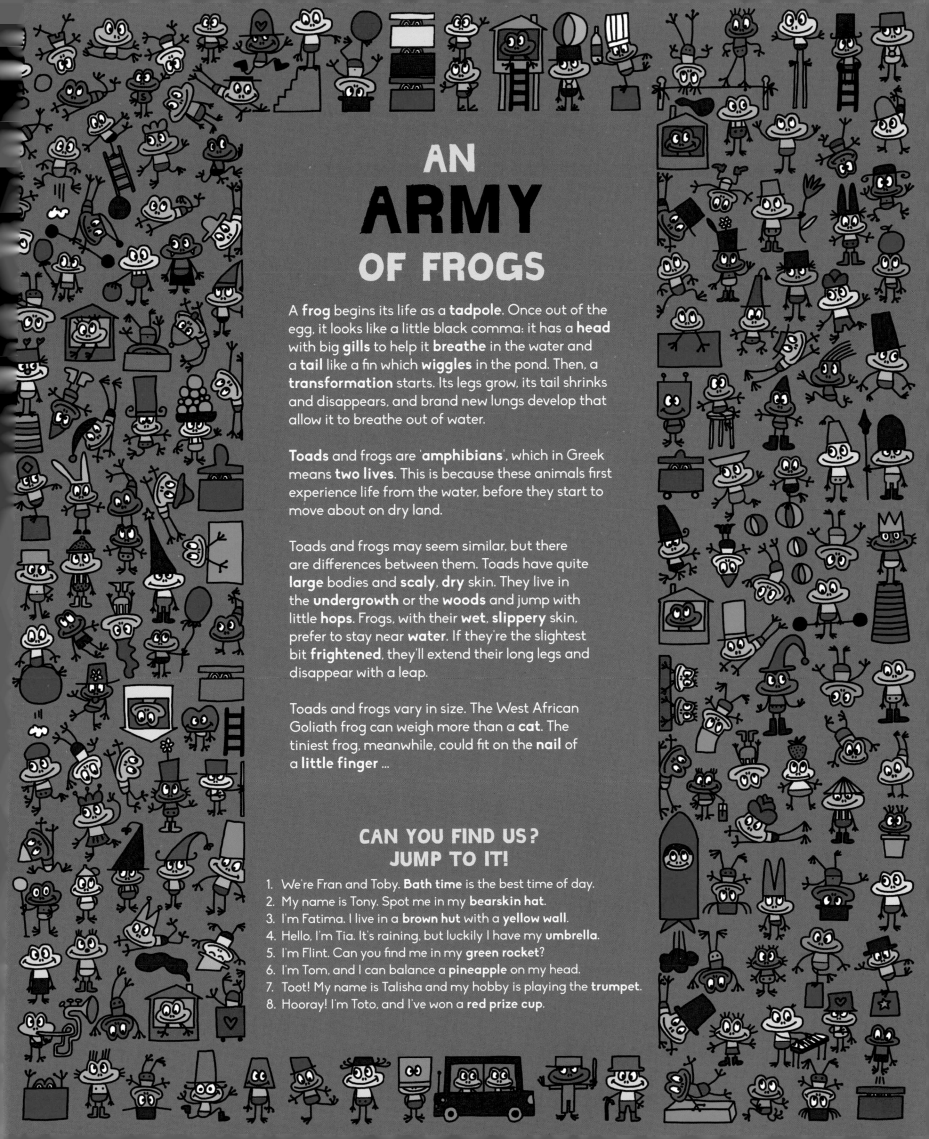

AN
ARMY
OF FROGS

A **frog** begins its life as a **tadpole**. Once out of the egg, it looks like a little black comma: it has a **head** with big **gills** to help it **breathe** in the water and a **tail** like a fin which **wiggles** in the pond. Then, a **transformation** starts. Its legs grow, its tail shrinks and disappears, and brand new lungs develop that allow it to breathe out of water.

Toads and frogs are 'amphibians', which in Greek means **two lives**. This is because these animals first experience life from the water, before they start to move about on dry land.

Toads and frogs may seem similar, but there are differences between them. Toads have quite **large** bodies and **scaly**, **dry** skin. They live in the **undergrowth** or the **woods** and jump with little **hops**. Frogs, with their **wet**, **slippery** skin, prefer to stay near **water**. If they're the slightest bit **frightened**, they'll extend their long legs and disappear with a leap.

Toads and frogs vary in size. The West African Goliath frog can weigh more than a **cat**. The tiniest frog, meanwhile, could fit on the **nail** of a **little finger** ...

CAN YOU FIND US?
JUMP TO IT!

1. We're Fran and Toby. **Bath time** is the best time of day.
2. My name is Tony. Spot me in my **bearskin hat**.
3. I'm Fatima. I live in a **brown hut** with a **yellow wall**.
4. Hello, I'm Tia. It's raining, but luckily I have my **umbrella**.
5. I'm Flint. Can you find me in my **green rocket**?
6. I'm Tom, and I can balance a **pineapple** on my head.
7. Toot! My name is Talisha and my hobby is playing the **trumpet**.
8. Hooray! I'm Toto, and I've won a **red prize cup**.

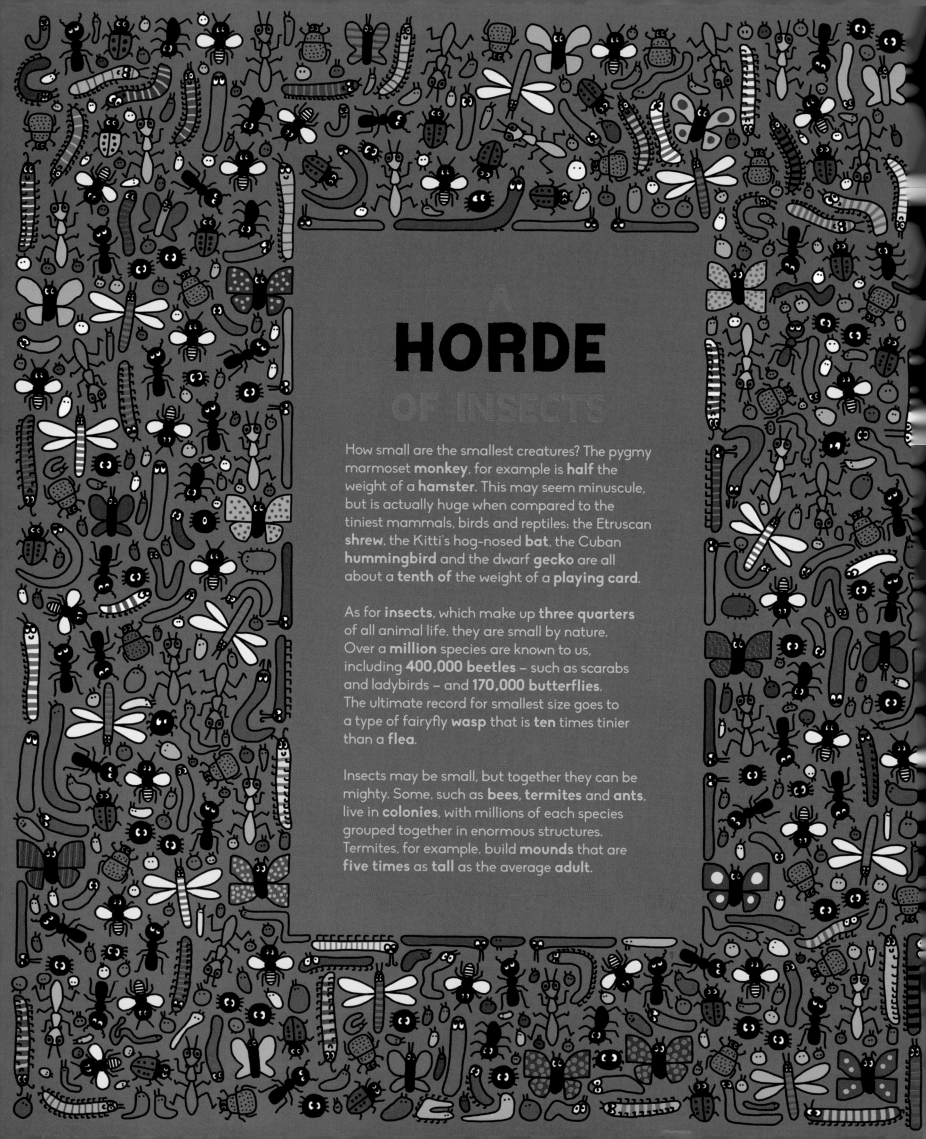

A HORDE OF INSECTS

How small are the smallest creatures? The pygmy marmoset **monkey**, for example is **half** the weight of a **hamster**. This may seem minuscule, but is actually huge when compared to the tiniest mammals, birds and reptiles: the Etruscan **shrew**, the Kitti's hog-nosed **bat**, the Cuban **hummingbird** and the dwarf **gecko** are all about a **tenth of** the weight of a **playing card**.

As for **insects**, which make up **three quarters** of all animal life, they are small by nature. Over a **million** species are known to us, including **400,000 beetles** – such as scarabs and ladybirds – and **170,000 butterflies**. The ultimate record for smallest size goes to a type of fairyfly **wasp** that is **ten** times tinier than a **flea**.

Insects may be small, but together they can be mighty. Some, such as **bees**, **termites** and **ants**, live in **colonies**, with millions of each species grouped together in enormous structures. Termites, for example, build **mounds** that are **five times** as **tall** as the average **adult**.

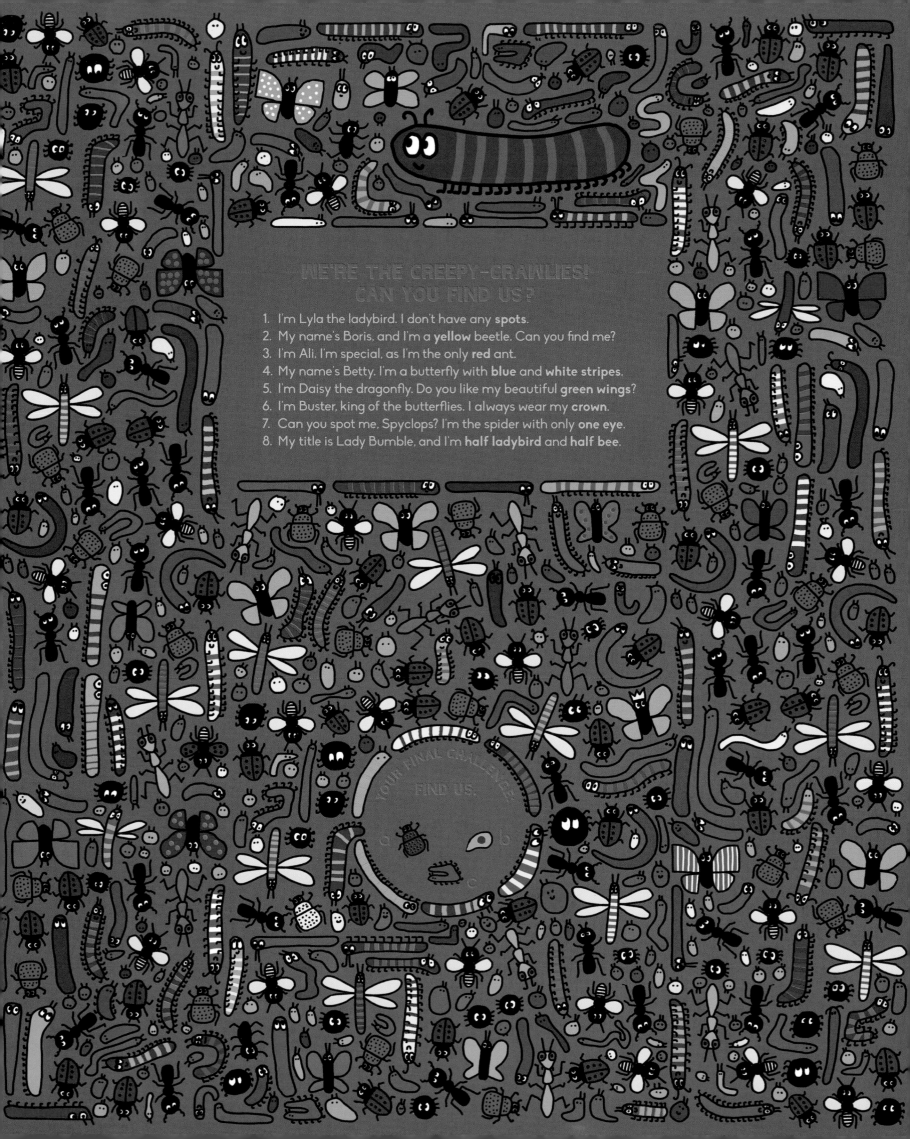

**WE'RE THE CREEPY-CRAWLIES!
CAN YOU FIND US?**

1. I'm Lyla the ladybird. I don't have any **spots**.
2. My name's Boris, and I'm a **yellow** beetle. Can you find me?
3. I'm Ali. I'm special, as I'm the only **red** ant.
4. My name's Betty. I'm a butterfly with **blue** and **white stripes**.
5. I'm Daisy the dragonfly. Do you like my beautiful **green wings**?
6. I'm Buster, king of the butterflies. I always wear my **crown**.
7. Can you spot me, Spyclops? I'm the spider with only **one eye**.
8. My title is Lady Bumble, and I'm **half ladybird** and **half bee**.

YOUR FINAL CHALLENGE.
FIND US.

A RELIEF
OF ANSWERS

AND SOME MORE FASCINATING FACTS!

A POD OF BLUE WHALES

There isn't a pair of scales in the world big enough to weigh a **blue whale**. Those giants are definitely the **biggest** animals alive in the world today, and probably the biggest ever. They can weigh the same as a **plane** and all its passengers. A whale's **tongue** weighs about as much as a small **elephant**, and its heart as much as a large **car**.

Yet, in the water, these huge sea mammals move gracefully and easily. They can **live for 90 years**, mostly alone in their watery kingdoms, powering themselves through the oceans with great **slaps** of their long **tails**.

Did you know that blue whales can swim while they're **asleep**? They shut down **half** of their brain, but need the other half **awake** to remember to **breathe**. When they swim to the surface for air, they shoot a tall fountain of **water** into the sky.

When blue whales get **hungry**, they open their mouths to suck up **krill**, which are tiny little shrimps. They can swallow **40 million** of them a day, and then they poop out loads of stinky pink poo ...

CAN YOU FIND US?

1. I'm Waleed. I'm wearing a shiny crown, can you spot me?
2. Hello. I'm Wendy – do you like my origami boat?
3. I'm Fred the fish, I'm very proud of my shark fin.
4. I'm Greta, the only green fish. Can you find me?
5. I'm Winston, the jazz trumpet player.
6. I'm Wan, I'm holding the anchor, but where am I?
7. My name's Wilma, I love my green hat.
8. I'm Bubbles the fish. I'm shaped like a little ball.

YOUR NEXT CHALLENGE.
FIND THESE, TOO.

- The blue whale is longer than **two buses** put together.

- Blue whales give off powerful, ultrasonic **waves**, which other whales can hear far away.

- The blue whale **call** is louder than a **jet plane**.

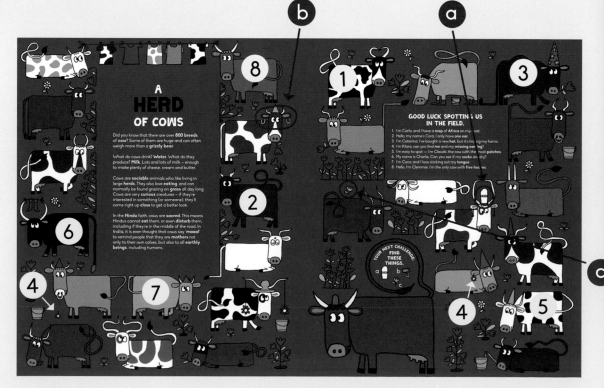

A HERD OF COWS

Did you know that there are over **800 breeds** of **cow**? Some of them are huge and can often weigh more than a **grizzly bear**.

What do cows drink? **Water**. What do they produce? **Milk**. Lots and lots of milk – enough to make plenty of cheese, cream and butter.

Cows are **sociable** animals who like living in large **herds**. They also love **eating**, and can normally be found grazing **on grass** all day long. Cows are very **curious** creatures – if they're interested in something (or someone), they'll come right up **close** to get a better look.

In the **Hindu** faith, cows are **sacred**. This means Hindus cannot **eat** them, or even **disturb** them, including if they're in the middle of the road. In India, it is even thought that cows say *maaa!* to remind people that they are **mothers** not only to their own calves, but also to all **earthly beings**, including humans.

GOOD LUCK SPOTTING US IN THE FIELD.

1. I'm Carla, and I have a **map** of Africa on my coat.
2. Hello, my name's Cora, I only have **one ear**.
3. I'm Caterina, I've bought a new **hat**, but it's hiding my horns.
4. I'm Klara, can you find **me** and my **missing ear tag**?
5. I'm easy to spot – I'm Claude, the cow with the most **patches**.
6. My name is Charlie. Can you see if my **socks** are dry?
7. I'm Coco and I love sticking out my **tongue**.
8. Hello, I'm Clemmie. I'm the only cow with **five hooves**.

YOUR NEXT CHALLENGE. FIND THESE THINGS.

- Cows **eat** for about **six hours** a day, chewing a total of **40,000** times.

- Cows can go **up stairs**, but find it harder to go **down**, as their **knees** don't **bend** in the right direction.

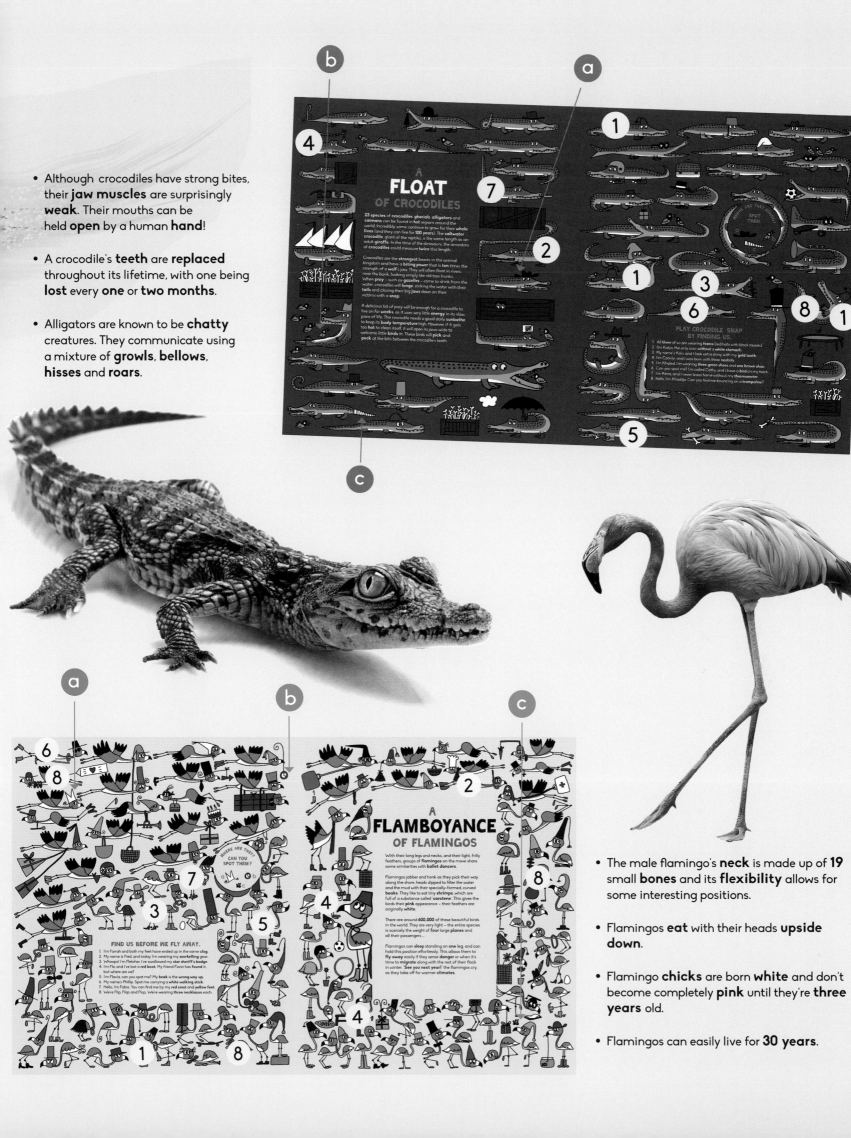

- Although crocodiles have strong bites, their **jaw muscles** are surprisingly **weak**. Their mouths can be held **open** by a human **hand**!

- A crocodile's **teeth** are **replaced** throughout its lifetime, with one being **lost** every **one** or **two months**.

- Alligators are known to be **chatty** creatures. They communicate using a mixture of **growls**, **bellows**, **hisses** and **roars**.

A FLOAT OF CROCODILES

23 species of crocodiles, **gharials**, **alligators** and **caimans** can be found in **hot** regions around the world. Incredibly, some continue to grow for their **whole lives** (and they can live for **100 years**). The **saltwater crocodile**, giant of the reptiles, is the same length as an adult **giraffe**. In the time of the dinosaurs, the ancestors of crocodiles could measure **twice** this length.

Crocodiles are the **strongest** beasts in the animal kingdom and have a **biting power** that is **ten times** the strength of a **wolf**'s jaw. They will often float in rivers, near the bank, looking simply like old tree trunks. When **prey** – such as **gazelles** – come to drink from the water, crocodiles will **lunge**, striking the water with their **tails** and closing their big jaws down on their victims with a **snap**.

A delicious bit of prey will be enough for a crocodile to live on for **weeks**, as it uses very little **energy** in its slow pace of life. The crocodile needs a good daily **sunbathe** to keep its **body temperature** high. However, if it gets too **hot** to clean itself, it will open its jaws wide to welcome little **birds** in. These birds will **pick** and **peck** at the bits between the crocodile's teeth.

PLAY CROCODILE SNAP BY FINDING US.

1. All three of us are wearing **fezzes** (red hats with black tassels).
2. I'm Katja, the only croc **without a white stomach**.
3. My name's Kim and I look extra shiny with my **gold tooth**.
4. I'm Connie, and I was born with **three nostrils**.
5. I'm Khaled, I'm wearing **three green shoes and one brown shoe**.
6. Can you spot me? I'm called Cathy, and I have a **bird on my back**.
7. I'm Keira, and I never leave home without my **thermometer**.
8. Hello, I'm Khadija. Can you find me bouncing on a **trampoline**?

A FLAMBOYANCE OF FLAMINGOS

With their long legs and necks, and their light, frilly feathers, groups of **flamingos** on the move share some similarities with **ballet dancers**.

Flamingos jabber and honk as they pick their way along the shore, heads dipped to filter the water and the mud with their specially-formed, curved **beaks**. They like to eat tiny **shrimps**, which are full of a substance called '**carotene**'. This gives the birds their **pink** appearance – their feathers are originally **white**.

There are around **600,000** of these beautiful birds in the world. They are very light – the entire species is scarcely the weight of **four large planes** and all their passengers ...

Flamingos can sleep standing on **one leg**, and can hold this position effortlessly. This allows them to **fly away** easily if they sense **danger** or when it's time to **migrate** along with the rest of their flock in winter. 'See you next year!' the flamingos cry, as they take off for warmer **climates**.

FIND US BEFORE WE FLY AWAY.

1. I'm Farrah and both my feet have ended up in the same **clog**.
2. My name is Fred, and today I'm wearing my **snorkelling gear**.
3. Whoops! I'm Fletcher, I've swallowed my **star sheriff's badge**.
4. I'm Flo, and I've lost a **red boot**. My friend Fionn has **found it**, but where are we?
5. I'm Flavia, can you spot me? My **beak** is the **wrong way up**.
6. My name's Phillip. Spot me carrying a **white walking stick**.
7. Hello, I'm Fabia. You can find me by my **red crest** and **yellow feet**.
8. We're Flip, Flap and Flop. We're wearing **three necklaces** each.

- The male flamingo's **neck** is made up of **19** small **bones** and its **flexibility** allows for some interesting positions.

- Flamingos **eat** with their heads **upside down**.

- Flamingo **chicks** are born **white** and don't become completely **pink** until they're **three years** old.

- Flamingos can easily live for **30 years**.

A WADDLE OF PENGUINS

Emperor penguins are the largest of the penguin species, especially at the start of the **breeding** season in **summer**, when they are at their plumpest. 25 penguins together are about **twice as heavy** as an adult **horse**, and each penguin is about the same size as a **seven**-year-old child.

On land penguins waddle along clumsily, but in the water they glide through the water with wings transformed into **flippers**.

When **winter** arrives, each female penguin lays an **egg**. She then sets off to find food for **weeks** at a time,

leaving the egg for her **mate** to look after. The male places the egg on his **feet**, keeping it warm in the fat folds of his **stomach**. And so begins a very long wait through the polar days and nights. A thousand dads stand together in a tight **circle**, braving the freezing **cold** and terrible **storms**.

While caring for the egg the male will not eat for **two months** and will lose almost **half** his body weight. When, at last, the female returns for the **birth** of the **chick**, the male can make the long march to the **ocean**. He will **dive** into the freezing water, looking for a well-deserved **fish** meal.

FIND US IN THE SNOW,
BUT DON'T GET IN A FLAP ...

1. Can you spot us? We're the **four dads** keeping our eggs warm.
2. I'm Paddy. I'm excited as the shell of my egg has just cracked.
3. I'm Paul. I've just come back from a **fishing trip** with a carrot.
4. Vroom! I'm Parminder. Do you like my **little red car**?
5. My name's Phoebe. Can you spot me on my **unicycle**.
6. I'm Piper. Can you spot the beautiful **star** on my head?
7. Hello, I'm called Polly. I'm off to my first **guitar** lesson, wish me luck.
8. I'm Pablo. What do you think of my new **trainers**?

- The emperor penguin can stay **underwater** for over **20 minutes** when it is fishing.

- Penguins **can** walk on the ice, but will often choose to **slide** on their **stomachs** instead.

- When little penguins want **food**, they will **whistle** to their parents.

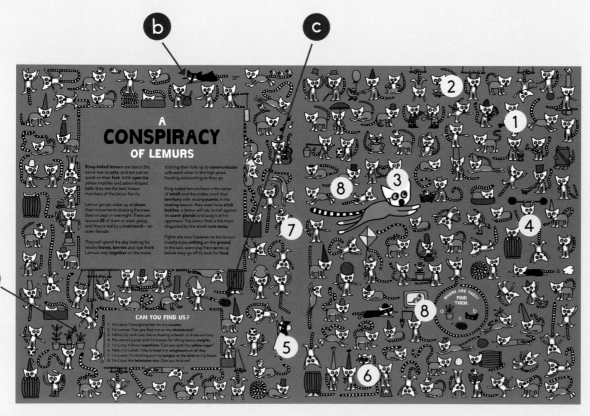

A CONSPIRACY OF LEMURS

Ring-tailed lemurs are about the same size as **cats**, and are just as quick on their **feet**. With **eyes** like yellow marbles and zebra-striped **tails**, they are the best known members of the lemur family.

Lemur groups wake up at **dawn**, their movements shaking the trees. They've slept in overnight. There are around 20 of them in each group, and they're led by a **matriarch** – an older female.

They will spend the day looking for tender **leaves**, **berries** and ripe fruit. Lemurs stay **together** on the move.

sticking their tails up to **communicate** with each other in the high grass, howling and purring as they go.

Ring-tailed lemurs have a fine sense of **smell** and the males mark their **territory** with strong **scents**. In the **mating** season, they even have **stink battles**: a lemur will rub its tail against its **scent glands** and wag it at his opponent. The lemur that is the most disgusted by the smell **runs away**.

Fights are rare, however, as the lemurs mostly enjoy **sitting** on the ground in the sun, warming themselves up before they go off to look for **food**.

CAN YOU FIND US?

1. I'm Lena. I love going fast on my **scooter**.
2. I'm Lamar. Can you find me on my **skateboard**?
3. We're Lily and Lisa. We're making a **heart**, to show our love.
4. My name's Leroy, and I'm known for lifting **heavy weights**.
5. I'm Lucy a lemur **superhero**. Can you spot my **yellow cape**?
6. Hello, I'm Leilah. I like to keep my **sunglasses** on all day.
7. I'm Louis. I'm sticking out my **tongue** at the **bird** on my head.
8. I'm Luca, the **television** star. Can you find me?

- Ring-tailed lemurs are known for **leaping** about. They can jump several times their **body length**.

- They have **four** fingers and **opposable** thumbs (like humans), so they can grasp things easily.

- Unlike most other lemur species, the ring-tailed lemur spends a lot of its time on the **ground**, looking for food.

- Jellyfish have no **brain**, **heart**, **bones** or **eyes**. Their **mouth** is found in the middle of their bodies.

- **Anglerfish** will **lure** in and catch prey who are attracted to the **light** coming off the top of their heads.

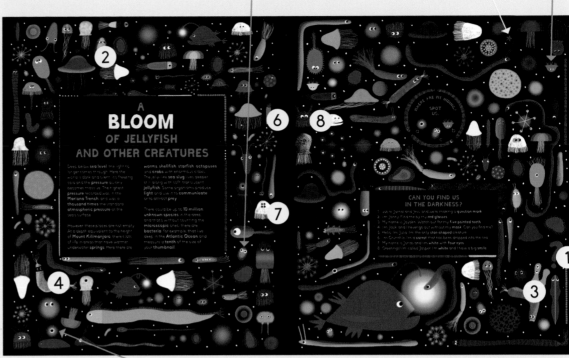

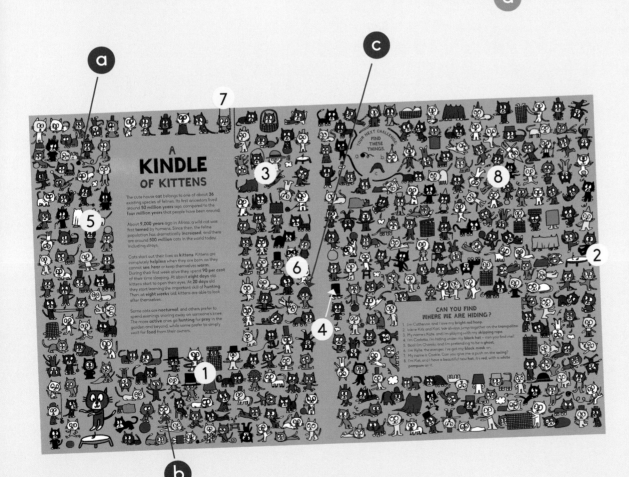

- Cats have an average of **244** bones and over **500** muscles, meaning they can twist and turn themselves into lots of different **directions**.

- Most kittens have **blue** eyes at birth, but this can change – their eyes will not be fixed until they are around **three months** old.

- A kitten **sleeps** for about **18** hours a day, while an adult cat will sleep for between **13** and **16** hours.

- The female frog **lays thousands** of eggs, which **hatch** after a couple of **days** or a couple of **weeks**, depending on the species.

- Frogs don't drink: they **absorb** water through their **skin**. For this reason, however, they couldn't survive in salt water.

- There is a tiny frog in the Amazon with **transparent** skin. You can see its **skeleton**, its **muscles** and even its **heart** beating.

AN
ARMY
OF FROGS

A **frog** begins its life as a **tadpole**. Once out of the egg, it looks like a little black comma. It has a **head** with big **gills** to help it **breathe** in the water and a **tail** like a fin which **wiggles** in the pond. Then, a **transformation** starts. Its legs grow, its tail shrinks and disappears, and brand new lungs develop that allow it to breathe out of water.

Toads and frogs are "**amphibians**", which in Greek means **two lives**. This is because these animals first experience life from the water, before they start to move about on dry land.

Toads and frogs may seem similar, but there are differences between them. Toads have quite **large** bodies and **scaly, dry** skin. They live in the **undergrowth** or the **woods** and jump with little **hops**. Frogs, with their **wet, slippery** skin, prefer to stay near **water**. If they're the slightest bit **frightened**, they'll extend their long legs and disappear with a leap.

Toads and frogs vary in size. The West African Goliath frog can weigh more than a **cat**. The tiniest frog, meanwhile, could fit on the **nail** of a **little finger** ...

CAN YOU FIND US?
JUMP TO IT!

1. We're Fran and Toby. **Bath time** is the best time of day.
2. My name is Tony. Spot me in my **bearskin hat**.
3. I'm Fatima. I live in a **brown hut** with a **yellow wall**.
4. Hello. I'm Tia. It's raining, but luckily I have my **umbrella**.
5. I'm Flint. Can you find me in my **green rocket**?
6. I'm Tom, and I can balance a **pineapple** on my head.
7. Toot! My name is Talisha and my hobby is playing the **trumpet**.
8. Hooray! I'm Toto, and I've won a **red prize cup**.

YOUR NEXT CHALLENGE:
FIND THEM.